AF407412

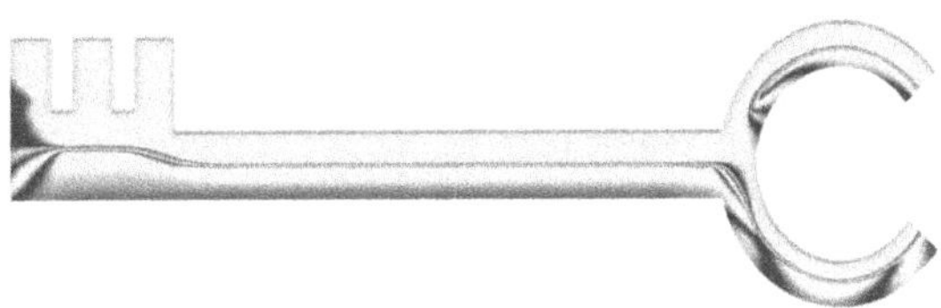

YOUR CONSENT

The Key to Conquering Sexual Assault

-REVISED EDITION-

JOYCE SHORT

ISBN 13- 9798218118167

Publisher: Pandargos Press
540 Main Street
New York, NY 10044

Design and Format: AuthorSupport.com

Contents

Introductions

When Bill Cosby's jury asked the judge for the definition for consent, he said, "That's a question that cannot be answered." Then he told the jurors to use their common sense. I was shocked. As a survivor, I was overwhelmed to hear that the law failed to define the very word that would determine Cosby's guilt or innocence.

When the important words in penal codes are ill defined, or not defined at all, neither society, the police, prosecutors, defense attorneys, judges, jurors, victims, nor offenders, know whether a crime took place. It is no wonder our arrest and conviction rates are abysmally low for sex crimes. *Your Consent – The Key to Conquering Sexual Assault* provides the clarity to put the entire justice system, as well as society, on the right page.

This book not only explains what consent actually is, it provides the concept to conquer the victim blaming and shaming the justice system hurls at victims. It is an eye-opener that can turn our human right of consent into a civil right, backed by law.

Joyce began her quest to correct the flaw in our justice system long before the #MeToo movement etched stories of sexual assault, harassment, and rape into the public's consciousness. I am proud to have joined with Joyce in the coalition she forged to create this vital, grossly overdue, and transformational change."

Andrea Constand, BA, Registered Massage Therapist
State's Witness: Bill Cosby's Aggravated Indecent Assault, 2018
Author: "The Moment: Standing Up To Bill Cosby, Speaking Up For Women"
Founder: Hope, Healing, and Transformation,
http://www.hopehealing.ca
linktr.ee/cryptobulllady

"It's absolutely essential that we understand and agree on what consent *is* and that we solidify a legal definition for consent in penal code for our courts to refer to. In this informative and important book, Joyce Short very clearly breaks down why we need this, and proposes an excellent and complete definition that would remove much unnecessary confusion in sexual assault cases and beyond. This small but crucial addition to our law books could make all the difference for sexual assault survivors as they grapple with legal proceedings, and raise the public's awareness in an effort to prevent all crimes involving sexual contact."

Miriam Haley

State's Witness: Harvey Weinstein's Indecent Sexual Assault, 2020

"New York and California are often considered the two most progressive states in the US, but in both locations, Harvey Weinstein's defense attorneys were allowed to rip apart each witness who testified about his sadistic, perverse actions. I know firsthand because I was one of those witnesses.

I learned the hard way that when someone overpowers you, immobility is a common reaction. Aggression by someone who actually knows you is shocking. No matter what the relationship has been, one can mitigate by trying to live through their conduct in the safest way possible; sometimes in ways others don't understand. Without comprehending trauma responses, victims walk away in a fog of self-doubt enhanced by society's negative backlash.

No one should ever be disgraced, humiliated, or shamed for how they survived that moment. All that matters is whether the accused did or did not have your consent. Without a clear definition, defense attorneys are free to re-traumatize victims in order to create a smokescreen to hide their client's wrongdoing.

Your Consent–The Key to Conquering Sexual Assault makes it clear that our laws are deficient, and provides the solution to hold sexual predators accountable. It enables victims to grasp when conduct is unlawful, and secure justice when they need to heal. This book can make a transformational change in our laws. Everyone should read it!"

Jessica Mann
State's Witness: 2020 Harvey Weinstein Rape by Coercion

"Your Consent- The Key to Conquering Sexual Assault is my go-to book that I always have on hand when I am speaking publicly and with legislators in our fight to change our laws. This book makes the distinction clear between *Coercion* and *Consent*.

Consent never takes place when "No," is not an option. Wielding power and misusing a power differential impacts people by coercion- the fear of the consequences if you don't comply.

Research shows that the first sexual experience by one in sixteen females is forced or coerced; but I believe it is far more prevalent. We need to educate the public and codify consent to prevent this violence, which causes poor mental and physical health outcomes later in life. It seems so logical yet people are surprised to learn that our states do not have a proper definition for *consent* in their laws."

Stacey Pinkerton
Cosby Survivor — Actor — Consent Crusader
Activist to Conquer Coercive Control
https://bit.ly/3UkiOJD

"We live in a misogynistic world in desperate need of champions for the rights of the oppressed. We need leaders who will rally against unjust systems and unite others to shape the government to reflect the interests of those it serves. Joyce Short is one of these champions.

Despite innumerable barriers working against her, Joyce is tireless in her efforts to educate and inspire others into action. She has fostered allegiances among survivor groups to ban together towards a common good, codifying consent. Once this goal is achieved, this book will finally become a part of history. Until then, we must continue to work together and bang our drums louder than ever to change the laws that support rape culture mentality. I give thanks to Joyce Short for leading the way."

Bird Milliken
Licensed Clinical Social Worker
Administrator: We Support the Survivors of Bill Cosby
https://www.facebook.com/WeStandInTruth/

Ms. Short's work on defining consent for our legal system, and in law, is both groundbreaking and remarkably logical. This book's definition of consent is based on the founding societal truths of our greatest thinkers: Socrates, Crito, Kant, Locke, and more. It turns the lens away from the present-day cultural system of victim blaming and shaming, and points it at the actor or perpetrator of the crime: "What did the perpetrator do to the victim?" Sexual assault, a crime of power — must be understood and prosecuted no differently than the crime of murder or any other crime. "Codifying consent," as Ms. Short proposes, supports one of the most fundamental truths of civil society — that every living human being has the right to bodily autonomy — to consent."

Susan and Alex Prout
Co-Founders, I Have The Right To,
Non-Profit Organization. www.ihavetherightto.org
Parents of Chessy Prout, Author: "I Have the Right To"
https://amzn.to/3VtErbQ

"I have been a detective for almost three decades and spent most of my professional life investigating sexually based crimes. I have seen firsthand the impact of how consent, or more importantly the confusion over consent, can determine the outcome of an investigation. Survivors suffer social torment when they are misjudged due to their actions or lack of actions, and are not believed by investigators and prosecutors.

In this book, Joyce Short explains why defining consent properly places blame where it should be, on the shoulders of the perpetrator, not the victim. Society desperately needs to end this victim-blaming, toxic narrative. This book provides the solution.

Joyce is also currently fighting to define consent correctly in the laws of each state. Most provisions about consent, especially for jury instruction, are confusing. Joyce fixes this dynamic by providing a simple definition that can lay the groundwork for change.

Steve Bishop
Detective: Colorado Law Enforcement

Joyce Short embraces the importance of defining consent. It is paramount if there is any hope of holding perpetrators accountable. Laws are expressed in words, therefore, precise definitions matter. Defining consent clearly in both penal codes and the Uniform Code of Military Justice (UCMJ) will eliminate using consent as a weapon to victimize the victim. Currently, UCMJ has only a partial definition for what consent actually means.

The rights of our people to have words clearly defined will deny no one equal protection under the law. This book sparks an important discussion about leaving no doubt in our minds with regard to the consent dilemma. It is a must read for all!

Marianne Bustin
Lieutenant Commander Aviation Maintenance Officer,
United States Navy (Retired)

"This is the primer for defining consent. Without a legal definition of consent, many rapists go free."

The Honorable Sally Siegrist
Indiana State Representative

"In this groundbreaking look at CONSENT, Ms. Short dissects the language in our penal laws that shape and promote today's rape mentality. Our current laws don't just fail us; they are the root of the problem!

Ms. Short is a true pioneer on this issue. While many organizations address social dynamics and healing, Joyce Short and CAN focus on the bedrock solution that will strengthen initiatives not only against sexual assault, but stealthing, image based sexual abuse, fertility fraud, coercive control–and anywhere consent is at issue - by embedding the accurate and enduring definition of consent into our laws.

This book provides an elegant, simple solution to shift courtroom behavior from victim blaming to holding sexual predators accountable. The original edition restored the self-worth and dignity of many survivors. This edition continues to fill this important role.

Nina Lucas
Chief of Staff
Lead Consent Outreach Ambassador for Pennsylvania
Consent Awareness Network

FOREWORD

My personal experience with sexual assault launched me on a mission to determine the cause of society's rampant level of sex crimes, and find a cure. My efforts date back to 2009 when I struggled to reconcile a devastating loss from the trauma I had suffered. Like with many sexual assault victims, I had buried my pain until reality overwhelmed me and destroyed the life I thought I had built.

In 2017, #MeToo burst on the scene. It enabled survivors to voice their stories and elevated the collective consciousness on how broad the problem of sexual assault and harassment actually is. It raised the specter of the poor response by our justice system. While #MeToo's impact on the public was and continues to be immense, stories alone do not create change. In words attributed to the late, great, Supreme Court Justice Ruth Bader Ginsburg, "We change nothing until we change our laws."

In May of 2018, at the Ursuline Academy in Wilmington, Delaware,

I presented my TEDx Talk, *When "Yes" Means "No" — The Truth about Consent*. I wrote the original edition of this book to convey greater depth on the issue of consent than I could accomplish in a seventeen-minute presentation. I've written this revised edition to give voice to the lessons our present system's failures teach us — as sexual predators dodge convictions and survivors are shamed in their pursuit of justice. My aim is to engage the public, provide a well-documented blueprint for change, and develop the momentum to make it happen. We can and must correct this toxic dynamic.

I created the Consent Awareness Network (CAN) to put my dream for an enlightened justice system into action and am truly grateful for the many survivors who joined hands with me to move our mission forward.

Consent is positioned squarely at the intersection between sexual assault, domestic violence, sex trafficking, fertility fraud, image based sexual abuse, and abortion rights, yet our laws fail to define this important term. For centuries generation after generation has tolerated its misuse. Defining consent properly in our laws will protect us today, and for all the generations to come. By reading this book, I hope you will discover the vital key that can solve the flaws in our laws and become a beacon for change.

Joyce Short

1

Why Is Sexual Assault Under Reported and Rarely Prosecuted?

In the quiet little seaside hamlet of Middle Township, New Jersey, on July 27, 2014, a forty-eight year old man — I'll call him Serge — raped his girlfriend on his garage floor. I'll call her Jessica.

Jessica was having dinner "out with the girls" that night when Serge called to check on her whereabouts. His controlling behavior and constant demands for "swinger" trysts had pushed her beyond her tolerance. No matter how many times she said, "No, that's not for me," he continued to badger her. She agreed to drive to his house, intent on breaking up and gathering her things.

She tried to keep her departure amicable. When he offered her a drink, she thought he was being cordial and accepted. A sudden churning in her stomach set off an alarm bell in her brain. Serge sat quietly watching as she struggled to stand and maintain her balance, as the room seemed to spin around her.

Recognizing something was horribly wrong, she stumbled to the garage where she had parked her car. She pressed the button to open the door. Serge closed it. She pressed again; he closed it again. Open, close, open, close... until her consciousness faded away.

Gradually, she became aware of her surroundings, ping ponging between an unconscious and semi-conscious state. She realized that Serge was sodomizing her and snapping pictures with his phone. The awful stench from her vomit, which lay just beside her head, filled her nostrils. Still, she was unable to move or protest.

When Serge finished, he hurriedly pulled a dress from a sack of property his former wife had left behind, and wiped himself off with it. Then he flung the dress into a corner. As he did so, Jessica summoned all her strength to flee. The only clothing Serge had left on her body was her halter-top. She was bare from the waist down. He had even removed her shoes.

The moment his attention was distracted, she struggled to her feet, fled from the garage, and made her way down the street. Serge jumped into his truck and chased after her. A young man in his twenties had pulled into a neighboring driveway and was getting out of his car. "Are you okay?" he yelled out, but Serge caught up to her, yanked her by her hair, and dragged her into the truck. Then he drove back to his house and held her captive overnight.

The next morning, Jessica pleaded with Serge and bargained for her freedom. He finally let her go. He threatened to come after her and her family if she reported the incident to the police. She had two sons and a daughter. Her youngest son still lived with her and her granddaughter often visited. She promised to comply. Once home, consumed by the fear of reprisal from Serge, she resigned herself to put the terror of the previous night behind her. She stepped into the shower and washed the residue of his filth from her body.

Although she just wanted to get past her ordeal, she found herself bombarded by the horror of the incident. Her brain repeatedly focused on how he had dragged her across the garage floor by her foot, "like a sack of potatoes." Her sense of intense defilement increased as her memory cleared. Eight days after the rape, she reported the crime to the Middle Township police.

The officer at the desk summoned a detective, a man she had gone to high school with. She felt totally embarrassed at having to divulge the traumatic details of the most intimate, dehumanizing event of her entire lifetime to a man she had known as they were growing up. The police made no effort to find a detective to substitute.

According to the Chief of Police in Middle Township, his staff was well trained to follow New Jersey's Sexual Assault Response Team (SART) protocols that were endorsed by the Attorney General. The standards in SART stressed providing the victim with "dignity, compassion, respect, and competency."

SART called for assembling a team comprised of a sexual assault forensic nurse, an investigating officer, and a confidential sexual assault victim's advocate. The police were not responsible for following SART beyond a five-day window, despite that there was no statute of limitations on rape in New Jersey and a five-year statute of limitations on Criminal Sexual Contact.

The police introduced Jessica to a woman they identified as her "advocate," but no one explained her role. Throughout their conversation, Jessica felt invalidated. In her words, "She was not receptive to what I was saying at all. She gave me no guidance, compassion, or reassurance. She surely didn't advocate for me."

Jessica explained her entire ordeal to the detective and the advocate, including all the physical evidence the police could find such as the photos in Serge's phone, the discarded dress, her vomit on the floor, and the eyewitness who saw her fleeing half-naked down the street.

The detective looked directly into her tear-stained face and said, "There is nothing we can do."

"Nothing?" she stammered in disbelief.

"Well, the only thing we can do is set up a phone call between you and Serge. We'll listen-in and record him. If he confesses to you, we'll go after him."

In crime-fighting circles, the detective's suggestion is called a "consensual intercept." Jessica understood that unless she got on the phone to confront the very man who had terrorized, horribly defiled, and threatened her with reprisal, the police would do nothing. She felt re-victimized and re-traumatized by the people she turned to for help. Hopeless and overwhelmed, she declined to arrange the phone call and left the precinct, as she fought back her tears.

Several days passed. Jessica heard nothing from the police or her advocate. No one checked on her or offered any form of support. Serge's words threatening her and her family if she went to the police was a frightening refrain playing repeatedly in her mind.

Serge had several life-long friends on the police force. Jessica was extremely anxious that he would learn she'd gone back on her promise of silence. Feeling vulnerable and alone, she contacted the police again. With her voice shaking, she explained that the risk to her and her family was too daunting for her; she was just "too afraid" to press charges. The detective asked her to come to the station.

The New Jersey authorities are supposed to issue an immediate temporary restraining order for rape victims under "Michelle's Law." They said nothing. No one attempted any form of emotional support. No one said anything about efforts the police would make to help her seek justice. Instead, the detective simply handed her a "Waiver of Prosecution" to sign. Without reading or understanding it, she signed where they told her, left the precinct, and battled against her fears and suicidal thoughts for well over two years.

During that time, she agonized over the assault, shaming and blaming herself for falling into Serge's trap. Days would pass without her being able to get out of bed. She sought help through therapy. She hoped and prayed he would not hurt anyone else. She moved three times to different states in a prolonged, costly effort to feel safe and put her life back in order.

SART describes that one of law enforcement's important roles is to ensure the safety and security of the public, but in Jessica's case, they left a dangerous man free to harm other victims. Unknown to Jessica at the time, two restraining orders had previously been issued against Serge. He threw his next girlfriend down a flight of stairs and dragged her out of the house by her hair. The police arrested him that evening, and released him the next morning.

Yet another victim — we'll call her Carolyn — stepped forward with a drug induced rape complaint that was similar to Jessica's. In Carolyn's case, Serge took her to a masquerade party in Atlantic City, New Jersey, for Halloween. When they arrived, he handed her a drink. That is all she remembers until she regained consciousness.

She found herself naked from the waist down and she had vomited on her shirt. Serge was dressing her. Other people around her were in various stages of getting dressed. She subsequently learned that the party they attended took place at a club for swingers. She reported the case to the police in Atlantic City. They did nothing.

Drug assisted rapes are among the most difficult to prosecute because the victims are unconscious and have spotty, if any, recollections. In addition to the sexual assault, however, Serge also stalked Carolyn and entered her house without her permission while her teenaged daughter was home alone. She sought a restraining order and subpoenaed Jessica, who had been silenced by a nondisclosure agreement that resulted from her civil case against Serge.

At the trial, Serge looked on smugly, chewing his gum, as Jessica testified under oath in open court. Her eyes clouded with tears and her voice cracked as she relived the horror she had faced. She disclosed that he had not only photographed her while raping her, but that some of the photos were in her attorney's file. The authorities subpoenaed those pictures. Still, they failed to arrest Serge for the rape of either woman.

Two years later, another woman filed charges against Serge. In a fit of rage that took place on his boat, he attacked her and broke two of her ribs. The authorities arrested him for aggravated assault, a crime that carried a maximum sentence of 10 years.

The District Attorney, who was keenly aware of all the prior accusations against Serge, allowed him to agree to Pretrial Intervention (PTI), a *diversion program* that grants parole and enables the record of the accused to be expunged. PTI is usually reserved for first time offenders of minor crimes, not violent ones. In May of 2022, Serge signed the agreement and pleaded guilty to the charges. He was paroled without serving any of his sentence, and avoided the fine.

Five additional victims have complained about Serge subsequent to the start of his parole. One claimed he drugged and handcuffed her. When she regained consciousness, a different man was on top of her. Serge is still at large and living on luxury yachts in Florida and Cape May County, New Jersey.

This story is typical of how victims are treated by the authorities. The press has focused abundant attention on celebrity, sexual predators like Jeffrey Epstein, Bill Cosby, Matt Lauer, Harvey Weinstein, Roger Ailes, and more. Their access to victims has made global, front-page news. But predators come in all shapes, sizes, and occupations. Without fanfare, their cases plunge through the cavernous cracks in our justice system, with little hope for accountability. Emboldened by their ability to get away with their crimes, they assault one victim after another.

The US Bureau of Justice Statistics says that victims only report approximately 35% of rapes, and less than 2% will result in convictions. The police take a greater interest in reports when the offender is a stranger, not an acquaintance. In fact, they rarely investigate rapes when the victim knows the accused. Unless the victim is badly battered, an individual case will get minimal attention. Our laws are not providing the protection the public needs.

In 2016, Captain Peter Rose, Commander of the 94th Precinct in Brooklyn, NY, cleared up any possible confusion over whether the police actually ignore acquaintance rapes. The police only investigated three of his precinct's thirteen reported rape cases that year. When a

New York Times reporter asked why, he said, "Some of them were Tinder, some of them were hook-up sites, some of them were actually co-workers. It's not a trend we're too worried about because out of thirteen, only two were stranger rapes." The third had been a case of child molestation.

Rose added, "They're not total abomination rapes where strangers are being dragged off the street; those are the troubling ones. That person has, like, no moral standards."

Sonia Ossorio, President of the New York chapter of the National Organization for Women (NOW), led a demonstration at the 94th precinct on January 10, 2017, objecting to Rose's remarks and the treatment of sexual assault victims by the New York Police Department (NYPD). Approximately one year later, the City Council of New York City demanded a public hearing to discuss police policy on rape with NYPD's top brass. The hearing called for testimony by the police as well as by victims' advocates and victims who had suffered humiliation and invalidation when they reported rapes at various NYPD precincts.

After providing their own testimony, each of the four high ranking NYPD officials left the hearing, without listening to a single word of the testimony that followed. By the time the hearing took place, Commander Rose had been promoted to Deputy Inspector, with a pay increase "in honor of his accomplishments as an executive," according to a police spokesperson.

Rose's comments underscore the reason why so few victims seek help from the police; they cannot count on them for an appropriate response. Instead, the callous invalidation they receive causes devastating retraumatization without a realistic expectation of justice. The system's failure to recognize the terrible harm the victim endured, no matter whether they knew or did not know the rapist, and no matter how the offender undermined their self-determination over their body, makes the victim feel isolated and alone, to a demoralizing degree.

WHY DEFINING *CONSENT* IS CRITICAL TO SOCIETY

The #MeToo movement has focused a glaring light on sexual assault. While it has raised awareness, it is an effort in desperate need of a solution. Defining "consent" in our laws is a critical key to that solution. In place of providing a clear-cut definition, individual states and jurisdictions use varied, sometimes partial, and sometimes incorrect language.

Not a single state or territory in the United States properly defines the noun "consent" in its laws. Other countries are no better. Seventy-six percent of US states and territories make no attempt at defining consent. The other twenty-four percent provide varied provisions that can often make sexual assault convictions impossible to achieve.

Provisions tell us how to behave using specific terms. Definitions tell us what the words and terms in those provisions actually mean. Penal laws have definitions sections for each type of crime as well as a definitions section for "general law," which applies to all crimes. The absence of a *consent* definition is a glaring omission that our legislators must change.

Increasing the level of confusion, individual jurisdictions have differing statutes to identify the crime of sexual assault. What constitutes acceptable behavior in one place can be a crime just a mile down the road in another. Our penal codes define sexual assault by specific offenses that lawmakers in that particular jurisdiction choose to prosecute, and ignore all other nonconsensual sexual conduct.

By picking and choosing specific acts, our laws fail to recognize the common thread that connects all types of sexual assaults, the defilement of the victim's body. Yet the defilement of one's body is exactly why our penal codes separate *crimes against the person* into a category for *sexual assaults* and yet another category for *assaults* that are non-sexual. Even though all jurisdictions separate these categories, some lawmakers and legal commentators erroneously argue that sexual assault laws exist only to protect against violence, but not to protect against the hideous soul murder of sexual defilement. All nonconsensual intrusion or contact with a person's reproductive organs must be recognized as a crime against that person.

Victims of violent rape grapple with healing their physical wounds and recovering from terrorizing trauma. But all sexual assault victims, no matter how they were defiled, face the emotional aftermath of depression, a sense of worthlessness, disorientation, feelings of contamination, self-blame, Complex Post Traumatic Stress Disorder (C-PTSD), anger, shock, helplessness, loss of trust, and more. Sexual assault victims can struggle for several years to become survivors. Many will need intense, on-going, professional therapy in order to put their lives back together, whether the offender used violence or not.

Failing to acknowledge that all nonconsensual sexual contact, by any means, is a sexual assault is like recognizing murders only when a person is killed in a specific way — like when they've been shot, but not when they've been poisoned. Imagine if we prosecuted theft only when the offender violently beats-up the victim to seize their property, but not when they defraud them or break into their house while they're on vacation. Just as no one has the right to murder or steal by any means, no one should have the right to defile a victim by any means. Nevertheless, that's not what our sexual assault laws say.

Our laws define murder as "the premeditated killing of another human being." This definition is not dependent on what weapon the murderer uses. Sexual conduct without the person's consent should be a crime no matter what malicious means the offender uses to undermine the victim's right to self-determination.

Nulla poena sine lege is one of the most basic principles in the rule of law. Wikipedia states: "It has been described as one of the most widely held value judgements in the entire history of human thought." Simply put, this ancient doctrine, dating all the way back to the Roman era, means that what is not expressly prohibited by law is permissible. As a result, without defining consent and stating that consent is required in all sexual conduct, our laws look like a Swiss cheese umbrella full of legal loopholes. Sexual predators slide right through those legal loopholes with no accountability or justice for their victims.

When a shocking sex crime hits the news without the means to convict, legislators will often try to plug up that specific legal loophole. Sometimes they succeed, and sometimes they fail. Even when they succeed, infinite amounts of additional legal loopholes remain uncorrected.

In order to protect the public appropriately, our lawmakers must create laws that recognize what consent is and clarify that ALL sexual conduct without consent is a crime. Doing so would turn our Swiss cheese umbrella into an umbrella with a thick coat of polyurethane.

HOW DID OUR LAWS GET SEXUAL ASSAULT SO WRONG?

Consent is an easily understood term that our laws have twisted and distorted out of shape because they are based on bizarre and outdated concepts like chattel. Chattel is the belief that a father or husband owns a woman's chastity. Women were expected to fight back with all their might to protect their virtue, a marketable commodity which becomes the property of her husband upon marriage.

Another driving concept which causes the "boys will be boys," rape mentality is the centuries old belief that a woman is a "temptation" for a man. This way of thinking provides the basis for objectifying and blaming the victim, even today.

A woman's right to vote was only recognized in the United States as recently as 1920. The concept that women can and should have the same privileges as a man, including autonomy over her body, is new. Our sexual assault laws, both in the US and abroad, have yet to catch up.

Our justice system's failure to recognize a woman's right to self-determination over her reproductive organs has enabled the recent overthrow of Roe vs. Wade by the Supreme Court of the United States (SCOTUS). Not only do our laws fail to acknowledge the importance of consent when engaging in the very act that creates pregnancy, many legislators across the US are demanding bans on a woman's right to determine the outcome of the resulting pregnancy. Men are getting away with rape while their female victims are being stripped of their right to escape the life-changing results of those crimes.

Legislators have made Band-Aid fixes to portions of sexual assault laws that miss the mark without the proper consent definition. Combined with the problematic sexist origins of rape laws, it is easy to understand why we have today's mess in which coercing, defrauding, or exploiting a drugged or intoxicated victim is largely ignored by the police. Even victims and the general public are confused and question whether sexual assaults are "just bad sex."

"Bad sex" occurs when a sex act fails to cause pleasure for both parties. Criminal sexual conduct, on the other hand, means that one person deliberately violates the sexual autonomy of the other.

Correctly defining consent will make it possible to appropriately prosecute nonconsensual sexual conduct, conquer rape mentality, and make the world a safer place. Consent is fundamental in all crimes of sexual assault, sex trafficking, domestic violence, and more. Consent applies in our human right to abort a pregnancy.

WHAT PREVENTS LEGISLATORS FROM ADDRESSING THE CONSENT FLAWS IN OUR LAWS?

Despite the obvious benefits, lawmakers refrain from correctly defining consent in penal code for several reasons:

1. Many legislators fail to relate to the defilement sexual assault causes. They dismiss sexual assault as "no big deal" unless violence is involved, just like Commander Rose.

   Before the 2016 sentencing of Brock Turner, a Stanford University student athlete found guilty of raping an intoxicated, unconscious, young woman named Chanel Miller, Turner's father pleaded for mercy. He claimed his son's conduct was just "20 minutes of action."

The concept that his son's 20 minute behavior permanently altered Ms. Miller's life was totally lost on him as well as the presiding judge, Aaron Persky. Persky said, "A prison sentence would have a severe impact on him. I think he will not be a danger to others," and sentenced Turner to a six month prison term. He served three months of his sentence. Ultimately, Persky was disgraced and recalled from the bench.

2. Most lawmakers continue to be men who, too often, are biased about a man's entitlement to sexual contact. They overlook the fact that men are also sexually assaulted. They dismiss sexual assault and the need for consent as a woman's problem. They cast blame on the victim for the "temptress" behaviors of wearing the wrong clothes, being in the wrong place, or having prior sexual relations with the accused. "Where is the woman's agency?" is an all too common cry that dismisses the real basis of consent, the influence the accused used to secure compliance.

In a recent radio interview, a "shock jock" asked me: "Doesn't a woman have a responsibility to protect her vagina?"

I was stunned. I attempted to respond that self-protection is an automatic reaction, unless the malicious influence of the offender prevented the victim's use of protection. Frequently, victims fear that fighting back will escalate the offender's attack. Freezing is as common as fighting or fleeing.

Jessica Mann, in her victim's statement at the sentencing of Harvey Weinstein, who had been found guilty of raping her by coercion, spoke about the effect of 'tonic immobility" in her case. Some victims will either consciously determine that fighting back will escalate danger, or may become so emotionally paralyzed that they are unable to move or speak.

The interviewer had consistently talked over me and answered his own questions. I recognized he was not going to listen to a reasoned response, so I quietly waited until he paused for a breath.

"Thank you," I said.

"Thank you for what?" he asked.

"Thank you for showing the world what rape mentality looks like," I said, and hung up the phone.

While both women and men can be victims of sexual assault, the Rape and Incest National Network (RAINN) states that 90% of adult rape victims are female. Because of this imbalance, sexual assault fails to generate the important attention and consideration it deserves from our overwhelmingly male lawmakers.

3. Lawmakers, judges, and prosecutors frequently ignore any attempt to expand penal law on the basis that doing so would overburden the courts. They prefer to confine sexual assault narrowly, thereby giving our laws the Swiss cheese umbrella effect. Their failure hampers society's understanding that all nonconsensual sexual conduct is a criminal act.

   The legal establishment claims that the cure, defining consent, is "too broad" or has "unforeseen consequences." In fact, the only consequence of defining consent is to enlighten society as to what constitutes a crime and provide the means to hold offenders accountable. Society needs the broadest protections that are possible.

   "Too broad" is a prosecutor's euphemism for "Criminalization costs too much money and doesn't create enough wins on our score card." Their priorities are in the wrong place. RAINN statistics show that 33% of raped women contemplate suicide and 13% attempt suicide. Rape, all too often, leads to the victim's death or extreme impacts on their lives. *The Journalist's Resource* estimates the economic cost of sexual violence to be "multi-trillion-dollars in the US." Overlooking the consent cure flies in the face of the real costs that prosecutors should address.

Defense attorneys push back using the smoke screen that defining consent will interfere with the defendant's right to the presumption of innocence until proven guilty. To the contrary, defining consent will streamline hearings to focus on what really matters: "Did the defendant use malicious influence to secure compliance?" It will prevent the victim-blaming defenses that attorneys wield like a weapon in a courtroom. What the victim wore or their previous sexual relationship with the accused will no longer be an admissible defense. The defendant's right to the presumption of innocence is unaffected.

Society elects lawmakers to create our laws. The legal establishment enforces the laws they make. While they see crime through a "how to prosecute" prism, society needs laws created through a "how to protect against harm" prism. Forming penal laws that protect the public should take priority. Society must demand that lawmakers accurately define *consent* in our statutes. Doing so will end the blame-the-victim nightmare that victims face in courtrooms and etch *consent* firmly into society's collective understanding.

Supreme Court Justice Ruth Bader Ginsburg, in her letter to the editor of *The Cornell Sun* on November 30, 1953, stated, "The criminal law not only reflects the moral outlook of the community, but may very well alter or create moral attitudes." Legislators who insist on narrowly confining sexual assault laws are withholding our constitutional right to equal protection under the law, granted by the 14th amendment of the United States, and reinforcing rape mentality.

4. Legislators are rightfully concerned that penal laws treat minorities unfairly. However, attempting to cure racial inequity in the justice system by closing our eyes to defilement is not the solution.

The US Department of Justice Statistics states that white males commit 63% of rapes against women aged eighteen through twenty-four. Minority girls and young women are at high risk for sex trafficking and domestic violence. Protections for this vulnerable section of society should be of paramount importance.

5. Some assault methods are so common and easily applied that society trivializes the defilement the victim suffers. The use of deception or a power imbalance that creates coercion causes severe harm to the victim, but our laws deliberately omit these covert ways to sabotage a person's free will. If the offender used these same malicious influences to take a person's property, our laws would readily recognize that a crime took place. In many states, the only recognized form of coercion in sexual assault is the threat of immediate and severe bodily injury.

Nay-sayers often argue, "Where do you draw the line in sexual assault?" They ignore that courts have tried cases for centuries where fraud is the weapon of choice for theft and other crimes. Even centuries-old Catholic Canon law addresses marriage fraud.

In all cases of fraud, including sexual assaults by fraud, requirements set the bar high for prosecuting offenders, thereby eliminating de minimis claims:

- There must be significant proof that the victim was deceived about foundational facts.

- There must be a reasonable basis for the injured party believing the deception.

- There must be proof that the deception, indeed, took place.

LESSONS FROM THE PAST

In ancient Rome, due to chattel, rape was only a criminal act when the target was a virgin daughter of a taxpaying citizen. Her consent was irrelevant. Rape was a capital offense against her father. Even if the daughter had agreed to sexual conduct, without her father's consent, the convicted man could be executed.

It was not a crime for the father to own and rape his slaves. Even in the United States, raping slaves was a common occurrence. Today we not only see raping slaves as morally reprehensible, we also see owning slaves as immoral. As Justice Ginsburg noted about the impact of our laws, abolition laws altered moral reasoning. We need new laws on sexual assault to reshape our moral reasoning the same way abolition laws did.

In the 2020 aggravated indecent assault case of comedian Bill Cosby, the first question the jurors asked the judge during deliberation was, "What is the legal definition for consent?" Because Pennsylvania's laws do not define "consent", all Superior Court Judge Steven O'Neill said was, "That is a question that cannot be answered. You're reasonable people. Use your common sense."

Fortunately, the foreperson for the jury was a woman named Cheryl Carmel. She was a cyber security expert and familiar with General Data Protection Regulation (GDPR), which contains a clear definition for consent. GDPR became international law in May of 2018.

Coincidentally, in the same month, I presented my TEDx Talk, at Ursuline Academy in Wilmington, Delaware. I was not aware of the GDPR definition for consent at the time; however, my TEDx Talk introduced the definition for consent in very similar terms, "Consent is freely given, knowledgeable and informed agreement, (#FGKIA)." In addition, the consenting party must have the capacity to reason. The similarity between GDPR's definition and my TEDx Talk demonstrates that the noun, consent, is a word with a singular definition and solid research will lead to the same conclusion.

The victim in the Cosby trial, Andrea Constand, testified under oath that Cosby gave her pills by convincing her they would cure her headache. Instead, they knocked her out. She was powerless to fight, flee, or do anything else. She surely did not have the capacity to reason. Armed with knowledge of consent's definition, which made common sense to Cheryl and the additional "reasonable" members of the jury, they unanimously found Cosby guilty.

As an advocate for defining consent, I was immediately struck with the consent issue in Cosby's case. Even prior to the trial, my coalition, the Consent Awareness Network (CAN) had lobbied several Pennsylvania legislators for change. We were eager to expand our outreach and had scheduled another legislative briefing to accomplish our goal. When I heard about the jury's "consent' question, I invited Cheryl to join us for CAN's legislative briefing in Harrisburg, PA's capital.

Five legislators and their staff gathered around the conference room table. I explained the problems with the state's current statutes and presented the "consent" solution. To drive my comments home, I asked Cheryl to explain what had taken place in the jury's deliberation. As she spoke, I watched the jaws drop of each person around the table. Not a single legislative participant was aware that PA lacked a definition for consent in its laws.

Cheryl, obviously, cannot be the foreperson for every jury. Unless we make the definition for consent clear to every jury, by turning our human right of consent into a civil right backed by law, justice for sexual assault victims will remain an unpredictable crapshoot.

According to Cosby's "common sense," *consent* meant underhandedly drugging women he enticed to his home and sexually exploiting their incapacity. Without the ability to hold everyone to a specific standard, legally acceptable sexual conduct is ill defined and, therefore, neither easily understood nor appropriately or consistently prosecuted.

Even the appeals judges on the highest court in Pennsylvania failed to hold Cosby's toes to the fire. Against strenuous opposition from three judges on the panel, the four remaining claimed that District Attorney Bruce Castor had given immunity to Cosby in order to compel his testimony in Andrea's civil case. The three opposing judges accurately pointed out that a district attorney lacks authority to provide immunity. Only judges can exercise that discretion.

The appellate court's judicial decision overlooked the fact that the only written record quotes Castor as saying that the Commonwealth of Pennsylvania retains the right to prosecute the case in the future. This disclosure is consistent with the limited rights described by the dissenting judges. No judge had issued Cosby immunity. The Supreme Court of the United States refused to hear the case. The Pennsylvania appeals court released Cosby from jail on their flawed technical interpretation of the law.

In June of 2022, Judy Huth prevailed in her sexual assault case against Cosby. She testified that he served her alcohol knowing she was underage and then molested her. The court awarded her $500,000 in damages. He has threatened to appeal the decision.

More trials loom on Cosby's horizon. Actor Lili Bernard is suing Cosby for raping her in an Atlantic City Hotel in 1990. She stated that when she told him she was reporting his conduct to the police, he threatened her career and her life.

On November 24, 2022, New York's "Look Back Law," the Adult Survivors Act (ASA), took effect. This statute allows victims to sue sexual predators for cases that are beyond the statute of limitations. Bernard is one of five women who recently filed against Cosby and multiple corporate entities who they believe knew of Cosby's behavior but failed to intervene. Actor and model Stacey Pinkerton has filed a separate and similar case.

Cases filed under ASA are hampered by the inaccurate view of consent in NY's laws. It's penal code states that a "no" or actions intended to convey "no" must take place. Conversely, its education law bases consent on requiring a "Yes." Neither of these conflicting statutes establishes what "consent" actually is, and can turn all the newly filed Cosby cases into a defense enabled, victim-blaming circus, like the recent Weinstein case in California. Far more to come on this important issue in the coming chapter.

2

Uncomplicating Consent

In 2014, President Barack Obama and then Vice President Joe Biden created the *ItsOnUs Pledge* to curb the rampant level of sexual assaults on college campuses. The very first line states: "Nonconsensual sex is sexual assault."

Today, both *ItsOnUs* and *End Rape on Campus* continue the effort to fight sexual assault at the college and university level. *I Have the Right To* (IHTRT), founded by Chessy, Susan, and Alex Prout, gal-

vanizes awareness for middle and high school students. Both Susan and Alex Prout have joined hands with CAN to define consent properly in our laws.

Unfortunately, the *ItsOnUs Pledge* is not law, even though it ought to be, and it does not clearly define what the noun *consent* actually means. Once again, society needs consistency to provide the "equal protection for all" granted by the 14th Amendment.

In 1962, the American Law Institute (ALI) published *Model Penal Code* (MPC) as an attempt to standardize laws across the US. Its *Consent Provision* says, "Consent is *ineffective* if induced by force, duress

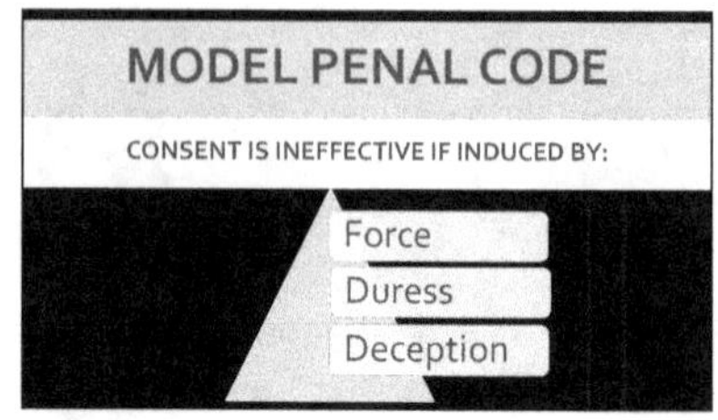

or deception." But "ineffective" only tells us what consent is not; it still does not tell us what consent actually is.

MPC creates a false impression. When you are maliciously influenced by force, duress, or deception, consent simply does not exist. "Ineffective consent" is an oxymoron. MPC also fails to consider the impact of the victim's incapacity.

The State of Missouri's penal code makes a far clearer statement than MPC. Their rape in the second-degree statute says, "*Assent* is not *consent* when induced by force, duress or deception." Unlike MPC, Missouri's law identifies that there is more than one kind of agreement, and that "consent," not "assent," must be present in sexual conduct.

Defining "Consent"

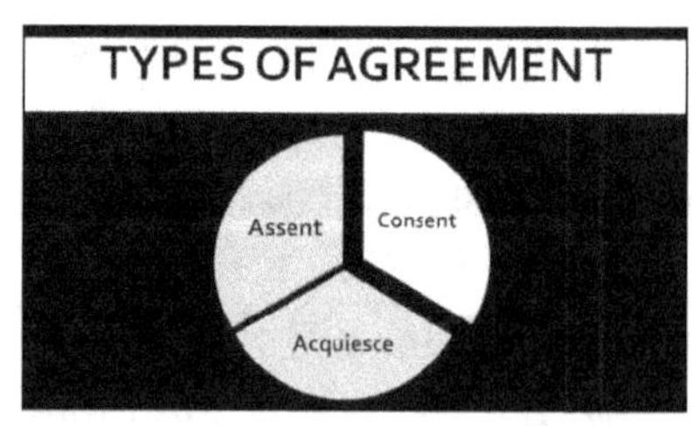

Consent does not mean "any old type of agreement." Three distinct types of agreement often take place in sexual conduct: consent, assent, and acquiescence. Of the three, only "consent" has the weight to make sexual conduct legal.

Widely recognized *consent* provisions support the concept that the definition for consent is a "Freely Given, Knowledgeable, and Informed Agreement —#FGKIA— by a person with the capacity to reason." Model Penal Code, General Data Protection Regulation (GDPR), which is international law, Nuremberg Code, the accepted definition that regulates medical experiments and research using human subjects, Catholic Canon Law, and Voting Rights Law all agree.

Nuremberg Code is responsible for your health care professional securing your consent form before injecting you with a Covid vaccination or treating any medical condition. If malicious influence caused you to sign your consent form, you did not consent even though your signature is on the dotted line. GDPR protects your internet data using the same principles.

The definition for consent does not change based on the subject of the agreement. Just as a rose is always a rose no matter if it's in your garden or in a vase on your dining table, the definition for consent remains constant no matter how it is used. The following statement describes consent in Nuremberg Code and shows how easily its language can be adapted for sexual assault:

> *"The person involved should have legal capacity to give consent; should be so situated as to be able to exercise free power of choice without the intervention of any element of force, fraud, deceit, duress, over-reaching, or other ulterior form of constraint or coercion; and should have sufficient knowledge (of the subject matter involved) as to enable him (or her) to make an understanding and enlightened decision."*

When applying Nuremberg code in medical experiments involving a child, the minor must *assent*, and their parent or guardian must *consent*. This is because the child has not yet reached the age of "reason." Even if they were informed and knowledgeable, because of their youth, they would not conform to the age requirement for reasoning ability. Accordingly, the *age of reason* is commonly referred to as the *age of consent*.

DEFINING "ASSENT"

Because of confusion, advocates try too identify consent in sexual contact as "express consent," "affirmative consent," "informed consent,"

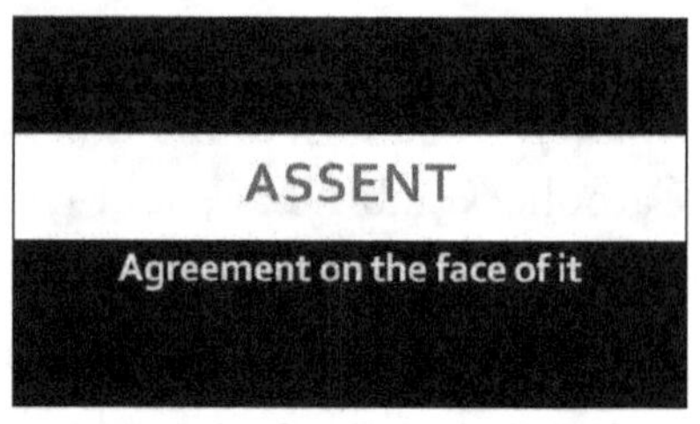

"enthusiastic consent," "knowing consent," and more. These concepts confuse and detract from consent's actual meaning because, by its inherent nature, consent is knowledgeable and informed. The term "informed consent" or "knowing consent" is like saying "a circular circle."

Just like there is no such thing as a shape called an "un-circular circle," there is no such thing as uninformed or unknowledgeable consent. There is, however, uninformed and unknowledgeable agreement. *Assent*, "agreement on the face of it," is agreement in which the person is not necessarily informed or knowledgeable.

When you nod your head or say "yes," you are assenting. When malicious influences cause your assent, such as force, fear, and fraud — I call them the three f-words that should never take place in sex — or when someone exploits your incapacity — the "I" word — you are not consenting. Hence, consent, not assent, is required for sexual contact.

The frequently used term "enthusiastic consent" is problematic for two important reasons:

1. The first amendment of the US Constitution protects our right to free speech. Our penal laws should not control the manner of speaking we use in the privacy of our bedrooms. Some people are more demonstrative and enthusiastic than others.

2. The determining factor in whether you consented is, "*What influence (causation) did the defendant use to secure your compliance?*" The accused always knows if they used malicious influence, so they always know whether you consented, even when you do not know it at the time. Statutes that determine consent by what a victim says or does hold that victim responsible for

their own victimization. Neither *Yes Means Yes* nor *No Means No* is a correct indicator of consent.

One early morning in 2016, as I sat reading my emails and drinking my coffee, I received a call from a reporter with *The Kansas City Star.* "Are you Joyce Short?" he asked.

"Yup. That's me," I said and listened.

He told me that the Federal Prosecutor in Kansas City, Missouri, had quoted from my webpage, now known as *ConsentAwareness.net,* in their indictment to lock up an offender they termed a "serial rapist." Their federal case was for financial and internet crimes, not sexual assault.

Although Missouri's penal law clearly states that assent is not consent when induced by deception, the Special Victims Unit Prosecutor, Jill Icenhower, failed to file rape charges against thirty-three year old Mario Antoine. He had deceived over thirty women into sexual conduct by pretending to be a porn videographer who was conducting auditions. He even drew-up elaborate contracts on a "Playboy Productions" letterhead that guaranteed the videos would be distributed only to "private international clients, not to customers in the United States." When victims discovered his fraud, he silenced them by threatening to send their auditions to their families and friends.

The Federal Prosecutor was incensed that Antoine had read my webpage, but proceeded anyway. They said searches on his cell phone "demonstrate his appreciation for the criminality of his predatory sexual behavior and demonstrate his willfulness in doing so." He was convicted of the federal charges and sentenced to a ten-year term, but the state of Missouri failed to charge him with sexual assault.

Larry Nassar, the doctor for the United States Women's Olympic Gymnastics Team, pretended he was medically treating his patients when he penetrated their reproductive organs for his sexual pleasure. They could only "assent," agree on the face of it, because they were not knowledgeable and informed. Nassar used the malicious influence of deception to undermine their self-determination over their bodies. Some of his victims were only thirteen years old.

Due to three separate convictions, each with multiple victims, one in federal court and two in the state of Michigan, Nassar will live the balance of his life behind bars. The judge who tried his case in Ingham County Michigan, and sentenced him to 40 to 175 years, the Honorable Rosemarie Aquilina, favors codifying the definition for consent into law.

Judge Aquilina says, "The legislature, and the supreme court need clear definitions of consent, both in the law and in the jury instructions. Without it, investigations are not completed, indictments are not made, and jury trials are lost—not because someone is innocent but because consent is not clearly defined. Once consent is clearly defined, the innocent, will stay free, the guilty will be convicted, and there will be fewer victims and less re-victimization."

Another example of using deception occurred at Purdue University in West Lafayette, Indiana. A college student named Donald Grant Ward was acquainted with the boyfriend of a female student who I'll call Anna. Even though she gave permission to release her name to the press, I prefer to protect her privacy.

Ward was among the friends that gathered one evening in the dorm room of Anna's boyfriend. Anna was an intelligent young woman who had been Valedictorian of her high school class just a few months prior.

As the evening progressed, Anna grew weary and climbed onto the top bunk of her boyfriend's narrow bed. Her boyfriend followed her up and settled behind her. She felt comforted by his embrace and drifted off to sleep with his arms wrapped around her.

The room was dark when Anna was awakened by a hand stroking her breast. The hand slid down her torso into her underwear, and engaged her in intercourse. Shortly, she needed to go to the bathroom and climbed off the bed. When she returned to the room, she found Ward, not her boyfriend, sitting atop the bunk and smiling down at her.

Bewildered, she decided to go down the hall to her own room. Her boyfriend was fast asleep in her bed. He had been uncomfortable in the narrow space of the bunk so he went to her room rather than disturbing her. When she told him what had happened, he went back to his room to confront Ward.

Ward readily admitted he had set out to trick Anna and knew he was doing so. Outraged by his behavior, she and her boyfriend called the police. Ward signed a statement admitting his actions. The police arrested him for rape.

Anna suffered through the grueling ordeal of the police investigation, prosecution, negative backlash from her peers, and the heartless, re-traumatizing, cross-examination by Ward's defense counsel. He insisted that assisting in unzipping Ward's pants, while she believed he was her boyfriend, proved that she had consented. The malicious influence of Ward's deception was totally irrelevant.

Because Indiana's laws failed to define consent, the jury acquitted Ward of the charges. No definition enabled jurors to distinguish between *assent* and *consent*. Moreover, in Indiana, sexual assault by deception or impersonation was not on the list of criminal sex offenses that the state would prosecute. Ward slipped right through the Swiss cheese umbrella that constitutes Indiana's penal laws.

Throwing fuel on the already scorching flames, the judge expunged Ward's arrest record, completely denying that Anna had suffered a defiling crime. Defilement by a despicable cur is one thing; the anguish of society turning its back on you is devastating and makes victims feel invisible, like they simply don't matter. Invalidation destroys the fabric of their self worth.

The Honorable Indiana State Representative Sally Siegrist spearheaded efforts to plug up the sexual assault by impersonation loophole in Indiana's laws and define "consent" correctly. She contacted me for help. She presented my TEDx Talk to her legislative committee.

Rep. Siegrist and I met with New York State Assembly Member Rebecca Seawright in the hopes of introducing similar bills in both New York and Indiana. I hoped having the bipartisan support of two legislators, a Republican from a red state, and a Democrat from a blue state, would be a game changer.

In March of 2020, Asm. Seawright introduced bill #A6540A, which is the very first bill to define the noun, *consent*, correctly in penal law. Senator James Sanders Jr. introduced companion bill #S6200A in the Senate. Both bills were introduced in the "general law" section of penal code so that consent will apply consistently in all crimes.

For too long, consent has been treated differently in sexual assaults than other crimes. By doing so, our lawmakers are handing sexual predators a "get out of jail free card." Enacting the definition for consent in general law, will clarify that the pivotal word *consent* is the same in each one of the 162 instances where it appears in NY's penal code.

Asm. Seawright held a press conference announcing New York's bills on the Day of Action for Sexual Assault Awareness Month in April, 2020. Both bill #A6540A and #S6200A are currently pending, and you can help pass them by signing CAN's support petition at http:// bit.ly/BillPetition.

When she lost her bid for re-election, Rep. Siegrist turned her efforts over to Indiana State Representative Donna Schaibley, who introduced House Bill #1549 in Indiana's legislature. Siegrist had revealed to me that the Committee Chair, Rep. Wendy McNamarra, said she did not see anything criminal in Ward's behavior and felt that protection was unwarranted. It came as no surprise to us when she quashed the bill.

A different type of legal loophole for *sexual assault by deception* popped up in Indiana in 2019. A fertility doctor named Donald Cline had artificially inseminated his patients with his own personal sperm instead of the sperm from the chosen donors. To date, research uncovered at least ninety Cline offspring, raising serious concerns about incest by unknowing siblings.

A Cline victim reached out to me to help her get consent recognized in Indiana's "Legislative Interim Study." I created a video presentation with two survivors from the Harvey Weinstein sexual assault case in New York. In addition, several professional advocates and sex crime survivors provided heartfelt, in-person testimony at the hearing. Once again, Rep. McNamara chaired the committee and shut down the effort, this time over the objections of bipartisan support from three legislators on her committee.

On March 11, 2022, Indiana's Governor signed Public Law #92. The press and legislative sponsors claimed that the bill defines "consent." Instead, it is a *No Means No* law that says that sexual assault takes place only by force or threat of force, or when the person does not know sexual conduct is taking place, when the victim is mentally disabled or deficient, or when the accused disregards the plaintiff's attempts to refuse sexual conduct. The reference to imposter rape, the use of imposter sperm, and the word "consent" do not appear anywhere in the statute's text.

In Texas, a thirty-six year old Dallas resident, Eve Wiley, conducted genetic research about her birth. Her mother and father had longed for a baby and sought treatment from Dr. Kim McMorries who had a stellar reputation for successful donor-conceived births. Her parents reviewed each donor's background data and selected donor #106.

Eve's father died when she was young. She missed having a father in her life. As an adult, when she learned of her birth history, with great trepidation, she set out to locate donor #106. She not only found him, but he was jubilant about meeting his daughter. The two formed a tight father-daughter bond. He even officiated at her wedding. They searched for additional offspring to add to their new family.

Due to a family health crisis, Eve needed to submit her DNA for medical testing. When she received the results, she was shocked to learn that Steve was not her father. Dr. McMorries was.

Eve brought her case to her legislator, Senator Joan Huffman. Unlike the stonewalling of Indiana, they succeeded in passing new legislation for Texas, which makes switching sperm during artificial insemination a "sexual assault by deception." Eve has worked diligently to secure similar statutes in several states. Three federal legislators are working on bills to take effect nationwide. One of the legislators asked me to analyze the best features of each bill in order to combine them into an all-encompassing statute. Eve and Jacoba Ballard, a Cline offspring in Indiana, have joined hands to secure nationwide legislation that will make fertility fraud a crime.

UNDERSTANDING SEXUAL ASSAULT BY FRAUD, DECEPTION, OR IMPERSONATION

In sexual conduct, clear legal language explains that both parties have the right to consent to the *action* itself and the *actor*. Tricking someone about the nature of the act, like Larry Nassar's crime, is *sexual assault by fraud in the factum.*

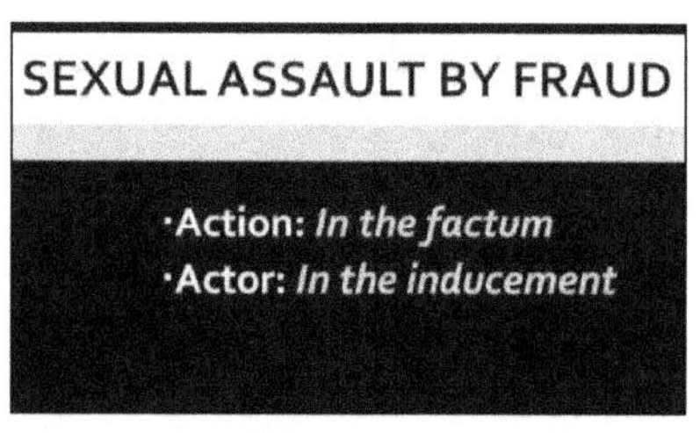

Tricking someone into a "Yes," when their actual interest would be a "No," about the actor, like what Donald Grant Ward did, is *sexual assault by fraud in the inducement.* Again, due to the 14th amendment, our laws must provide protection unilaterally. Fraud is no exception.

Fraud that is used to undermine your self-determination over your sexual autonomy should be recognized as a sexual assault. It is a covert weapon of choice for underhanded, sexual predators. The widely accepted steps for committing fraud in all crimes throughout the US are:

1. The offender deceives.
2. The offender knows they are deceiving.
3. The offender intends for the victim to believe their deception.
4. The victim, indeed, believes their deception.
5. The victim suffers harm resulting from believing their deception.

Lying or deceiving to attract someone's romantic interest is not a crime. Romantic deceptions are so abundant on the internet that they have a special name, "Catfishing." If the offender causes the victim significant emotional harm, they could sue for personal injury or emotional distress. First, they would need to find an attorney to take their case and would have to pay a retainer and additional costs as their case progressed. Unless the offender had sufficient assets to warrant a "pay day" for their attorney, securing legal counsel would be a challenge. Misusing the internet to conduct emotional upheaval in people's lives should be a crime.

If the offender fails to straighten out their lies before they engage in sexual contact, their conduct crosses the line from seduction to sexual assault. Prosecuting crimes does not require the victim to secure legal counsel, although many victims do. The prosecutor tries the case as an offense against the state or jurisdiction, and the victim becomes the state's key witness.

Defining "Acquiescence"

Our states prohibit prison guards from engaging in sexual contact with prisoners. Their relationship is considered a "power differential." The guard controls the prisoner's well-being; yet RAINN reports that jail or prison staff commit 60% of sexual violence against inmates.

When a person misuses a power differential to induce sexual contact, they are coercing the victim who acquiesces — agrees out of fear. Ironically, many of the states with laws that recognize the inherent power differential in guard/prisoner relationships fail to recognize how "acquiescence" applies in other cases of coercion and undue influence.

Harvey Weinstein was a powerful movie producer when, according to at least eighty complainants, he exposed himself and demanded sexual conduct. Some of his victims said that he forced them. Others were afraid he would destroy their careers if they refused his demands.

Agreement under duress is acquiescence, not consent, no matter what type of fear is used. Currently, many states only prosecute instilling fear when the offender threatens violence.

Weinstein and his team of attorneys, headed by Donna Rotunno, argued that his victims all consented. She contended that their behavior, after the fact, was factual proof they had consented. She stated that he was a "victim" of the #MeToo movement.

A return to normalcy motivates many victims of sexual abuse or assault. The same fear of loss during the incident can continue to motivate the victim after the incident. Not only did Weinstein's victims think the authorities would do nothing for them, they also thought that pretending the incident never happened would help return them to normalcy.

Rotunno derided the Prosecutor, Assistant District Attorney Joan Illuzzi, for "stripping women of common sense, autonomy and responsibility." She failed to acknowledge that coercion causes acquiescence, not consent. She was oblivious to the defilement victims experience in misuse of a power differential to secure sexual contact.

Dr. Barbara Ziv, a highly recognized forensic psychologist, testified as an expert witness, stating that studies have shown there is no continuity in how victims will react. Their behavior, after–the-fact, does not indicate whether or not a crime took place.

Dr. Ziv's responsibility as an expert witness was to present impartial factual data about victim behavior in general, not the behavior of the specific witnesses. Rotunno attempted to impugn Ziv's credibility by repeatedly asking if she had interviewed the witnesses. In her closing argument, she accused Illuzzi of creating "theatre," as she parroted the words of Atticus Finch, the principle character in the play, *To Kill a Mockingbird*.

The morning after Rotunno's summation, the press lined up on one side of the corridor to the courtroom, and the public, including me, lined up on the other side. All the attorneys and staff for the prosecutor and defense travelled down the passageway between us. As she walked, reporters shouted their questions. "How do you think your summation went yesterday?" one asked.

"I thought it was great," she responded.

"Great if you're Atticus Finch," I remarked.

She flashed a wry smile as she went by.

Five years prior to Weinstein's trial, New York State had passed its *Yes Means Yes* bill into education law. This law provided no answer when, just like in Cosby's case, Weinstein's jurors asked Judge James Burke for the definition of consent. Because in New York, just like in Pennsylvania, there is no definition for consent in penal code, Judge Burke responded, "Use your common sense."

The charges against Weinstein, who was sixty-seven at the time, were Predatory Sexual Assault, which carried a life sentence, Rape in the Third Degree, and Criminal Sexual Assault. The jury convicted him of Rape in the Third Degree and Criminal Sexual Assault. Combined, his sentence could have amounted to twenty-nine years. He was sentenced to twenty-three.

At his sentencing hearing, Weinstein seemed shocked by his conviction. "But I never forced anyone," he said, "I didn't have to." He was oblivious to the concept that imposing sex by instilling fear was a sexual assault. The media completely missed this important point. Without media focus, the coercion lessons learned by locking up Weinstein went unnoticed.

Weinstein said, "It's just, I'm totally confused and I think all men are confused about these issues." Our legislators need to heed his claim of "confusion," and make *consent* abundantly clear.

During his New York trial, the state of California filed charges against Weinstein for two counts of rape and five counts of sexual assault. Pseudonyms protected the identities of most of the victims, but Jane Doe #4 agreed to be identified by her actual name, Jennifer Siebel Newsom, the wife of California Governor Gavin Newsom. She initially believed her involvement with the case was as support for the other victims, but the prosecution pressed charges on her accusations.

The trial included the cases of four victims, a model, dancer, massage therapist, and Ms. Siebel Newsom, a producer.

According to Siebel Newsom, she and Weinstein met in 2005 at the Toronto Film Festival. She was building her career at the time. He called her in Los Angeles to arrange a meeting to help further her efforts. Instead, she described in open court that he seized the opportunity to sexually assault her.

Weinstein's attorney, Mark Werksman, formerly a Deputy District Attorney and Assistant US Attorney, employed the victim blaming tactics that California's law enables. He focused on Siebel Newsom's behavior in order to blur the line between cause and effect:

1. He attempted to discredit her testimony by presenting that some years later, she corresponded with Weinstein by email.

2. He attempted to defame her by claiming, "She's made herself a prominent victim in the #MeToo movement..... otherwise, she'd be just another bimbo who slept with Harvey Weinstein to get ahead in Hollywood."

3. He demanded that she fake an orgasm during her testimony. She had explained she had done so to speed Weinstein's completion during his assault. She was stunned by his request. "This isn't 'When Harry met Sally,'" she said, as she burst into tears.

Her comment harkened back to the iconic, 1989 movie scene when actor Meg Ryan, seated in a deli, faked an orgasm. Producer Rob Reiner's mother delivered the memorable one-liner "I'll have what she's having." Siebel Newsom's one-liner could go down in history as a pivotal statement helping society recognize that the conduct of the accused, not the victim, should determine guilt or innocence in a court of law.

Werksman's cringe-worthy conduct was allowable in the courtroom because California's 2014, *Yes Means Yes* law, signed by then Governor Jerry Brown, enabled it. While the present Governor, Gavin Newsom praised the bravery of the witnesses for coming forward, society needs changes in the laws that enable victim-blaming and shaming defenses. "Positive cooperation in act or attitude pursuant to the exercise of free will," the wording of CA's current law, supports the defense attorney's mistreatment of the victim. Defining consent properly would create the needed, transformational change.

Model Jury Instructions, informed by the correct definition for consent, would prohibit a Werksman-like cross-examination, rendering it inadmissible. Most importantly, correctly defining consent will diminish the quantity of sex crimes by creating consistent, real, and equal protection under the law.

On the tenth day of jury deliberations, the California trial ended in a split decision, highlighting the ambiguous nature of the state's laws. "They deserve better than what the system has given them," said George Gascón, Los Angeles County District Attorney. While correctly stated, the jury is out on whether this important recognition will lead California's legislators to create change.

Of the seven counts charged, Weinstein was pronounced guilty of three: rape, forcible oral copulation, and sexual penetration by a foreign object, against one out of four of the key witnesses. California's sentence, which begins when New York's sentence ends, will keep Weinstein in jail for the rest of his life.

The jury acquitted on one count of sexual battery and could not reach a decision on three other counts, including the charges made by Siebel Newsom. Media speculation for the jury's conflict blamed her after-the-fact contact with Weinstein as the reason. The state has the option to continue pursuing her claims.

If consent were clearly defined in law and addressed correctly in model jury instructions, sex crime hearings would examine the type of influence the accused used to compel compliance, not the non-related contact between the parties. Instead, because of Werksman's highly publicized, grueling cross examination, which Newsom subsequently characterized as "sexism, misogyny, and bullying," and the mixed verdict that rendered justice to only 25% of the complainants, victims will be less hopeful for support if they report. Society desperately needs to change this harmful dynamic.

Another type of acquiescence occurs when the victim is in a compromised state due to drugs or alcohol. They lack the mental clarity to process information. How they become incapacitated should not matter, but many states only prosecute offenders when they cause the victim's incapacity. If they steal your wallet while you are drunk or drugged, however, they are committing a crime.

The New York State Senate recently passed a bill to make anyone who is incapacitated by drugs or alcohol off limits for sexual contact. The New York State Assembly failed to support this bill. Although crimes against the person are considered more serious than crimes against property, lawmakers seem to have difficulty wrapping their heads around the fact that a sexual intrusion or violation of your body causes defilement whether you knew it was happening at the time, or found out after the fact.

CAN is working with Cosby survivor Stacey Pinkerton to push for consent legislation in the state of Arkansas. She is also fighting to create society's recognition of workplace coercion, and establish that no one can possibly be consenting when "No," is not an option.

Arkansas State Representative Robin Lundstrum and Senator Clint Penzo introduced AR Bill #1141, on Tuesday, June 17, 2023, to define consent in Arkansas's penal laws using CAN's #FGKIA model. You can support passage of this bill into law by signing CAN's petition at http://bit.ly/BillPetition.

State of Arkansas, 94th General Assembly A Bill
Regular Session, 2023 HOUSE BILL 1141

AN ACT TO DEFINE THE TERM "CONSENT" REGARDING SEXUAL OFFENSES WITHIN THE ARKANSAS CRIMINAL CODE; AND FOR OTHER PURPOSES.

BE IT ENACTED BY THE GENERAL ASSEMBLY OF THE STATE OF ARKANSAS:

SECTION 1. Arkansas Code § 5-14-101, concerning definitions regarding sexual offenses under the Arkansas Criminal Code, is amended to add an additional subdivision to read as follows:

"Consent" means a freely given, knowledgeable, and informed agreement without malicious actions or influences, including without limitation:

(A) Physical force;
(B) Coercion;
(C) Fear;
(D) Fraud;
(E) False identity; or
(F) Exploitation of a person's incapacity.

CONSENT, THE NOUN VS. *TO CONSENT,* THE VERB

The verb, *to consent,* the infinitive form, rests entirely on the definition of the noun, *consent.* Just as a chef cannot "plate" *(v)* a meal without arranging it on a "plate" *(n)*, or a baseball pitcher cannot "strike out" *(v)* a player without throwing a "strike" *(n)*, a person cannot convey "consent" *(v)* without the noun "consent" being present.

- *Freely given, knowledgeable and informed agreement by a person with the capacity to reason* is the definition for the noun, "consent."
- *To convey consent to another person or entity* is the definition for the verb "to consent."

When a person "agreed" because they were forced, scared, tricked, or if they were incapacitated, no matter what they said or did, they were not "consenting."

New York State's education law on consent claims that "words and actions" determine whether consent is present. In fact, this statute requires all 240 colleges and universities within the state to include this *Yes Means Yes* concept in their Codes of Conduct. Failure to do so will result in withdrawal of NY State's aid or assistance. It is little wonder that Governor Andrew Cuomo, who signed this flawed concept into law, resigned his office in disgrace due to charges of his personal sexual impropriety against women.

By defining consent accurately, we see that "words and actions" are a conveyance. In order for those words and actions to convey consent, the noun "consent" must actually be taking place. The influence by the accused, not the resultant words and actions of their target, determines if consent occurred.

REVOKE VS. REVERSE AND RETRACT

Consent can be revoked at any time while the agreed-to conduct is taking place because consent must always be *freely given*. When a person changes their mind during sexual conduct, all sexual contact must cease, or the specific objected-to act must cease.

Retract, reverse, and revoke are similar but not the same and are often confused in discussions about consent. Retract, in addition to "withdraw," can also mean "to go back on." Reverse means to change to the opposite direction. Revoke is the term that best establishes that a party is entitled to cease consenting while the conduct is taking place.

While this similarity might seem like frivolous hair-splitting, one never knows what interpretation an attorney, judge, or jury may attach to the words in a statute. In order to prevent mistakes, the wording must be as unambiguous as humanly possible.

When both parties achieved freely given knowledgeable and informed agreement at the time the conduct occurred, they cannot subsequently go backwards in time and retract or reverse the decision they made.

Having second thoughts (regrets) on whether you made a wise

choice for yourself is not at all the same as discovering, after the fact, that you were maliciously influenced at the time you made your decision. If after the fact, the victim recognizes they complied due to force, fear, fraud, or the exploitation of their incapacity, indeed, the accused did not have the victim's consent at the time the incident took place.

Alan Jackson, another of Harvey Weinstein's attorneys in his 2022 California trial said, "Regret is not the same thing as rape. And it's important we make that distinction in this courtroom."

While he was correct that regret is not rape, he confused *regret* with *recognition*. He used this false narrative to cloud the jury's perception. The recognition that you have been sexually assaulted, whether in the moment or some time thereafter, is a horrifying, and often overwhelming awareness.

MUTUAL VS. SIMULTANEOUS

Some states describe consent as "mutual." In fact, consent is a highly individual, autonomous attitude that results from influence. All parties are entitled to their individual choices for whatever reasons are pertinent to them. No one, including a sex worker, is ever required to have sexual contact with another person. Everyone can autonomously change their mind.

Because consent is simultaneous and not mutual, the person wanting to stop sexual contact or a sexual act does not need the other person's permission to do so. Considering consent as "mutual" flies in the face of each person's autonomous right to revoke.

3

How Should Consent Apply in Penal Code?

All violent crimes, and crimes where weapons are used, are "aggravated offenses." The sentence is harsher for violent than non-violent crimes. Harvey Weinstein received a three-year sentence for raping Jessica Mann by coercion, regardless that Jessica credibly testified to Weinstein's forcible conduct. He was sentenced to twenty years for the violent sexual assault of Miriam Haley.

Our laws should be clear that violent rape is an aggravated form of sexual assault, but all sexual assaults, whether committed in a violent or non-violent manner, are the nonconsensual exploitation of a person's reproductive organs, and should be recognized as crimes.

If an offender beats you up to steal your money, they are committing an aggravated offense. The punishment is more severe than if they break into your car to take your wallet, or if they defraud you of your property. Wealth manager Bernie Madoff died in jail while serving his 150-year sentence for theft by using the fraud of an elaborate Ponzi scheme. Even though his victims enthusiastically handed him their money, they were convinced to do so by his deception.

Using any type of device or manipulation to undermine your self-determination over your property is a punishable offense. However, sexual assault laws focus on force and threat of force, ignoring other malicious influences. Obtaining sexual contact by wielding the coercion of a power differential or concerns over losing one's career, scholarship, or home, are not treated as a crime in most states.

Catholic Canon Law has considered the use of fraud in theft, "without consent," for centuries. Every day, our present justice system locks up offenders when they use malicious influence to steal because we recognize that tricking a person to take property is a crime.

When a person deceives us with a foundational fact, and there is clear evidence they have done so, when a "reasonable person" would have been tricked," and when there is sufficient evidence that the crime took place, the offender should be prosecuted for sexual assault, just as they would be prosecuted for theft.

We cannot and should not base recognition of what constitutes a crime on how easy or difficult prosecuting any specific case may be. We can and should base recognition of a crime on whether the behavior causes harm to victims. The Federal Bureau of Investigation's tracking of crimes and arrests shows that only approximately 41% of crimes lead to an arrest. In fact on December 2, 2022, station KSAT 12 in San Antonio, Texas, announced a 35% arrest rate for local murders for the year. Their statistic is similar to other jurisdictions across the US. We recognize the crime of murder, regardless that the vast majority of murder cases are not prosecuted.

WHAT PENALTIES ARE APPROPRIATE FOR SEXUAL PREDATORS?

While all stealing is a crime, sentencing depends on the method the offender used and extent of the harm. Sentencing for sexual assaults should vary according to the method used, with violent sexual assaults punished more harshly than non-violent sexual assaults. Violation of a person's reproductive organs, regardless of the degree, is an assault on the victim.

- A violent form of sexual assault, a sexual assault using a weapon, or a sexual assault in which the victim is coerced through threats of violence, should be punished as a Class A Felony.

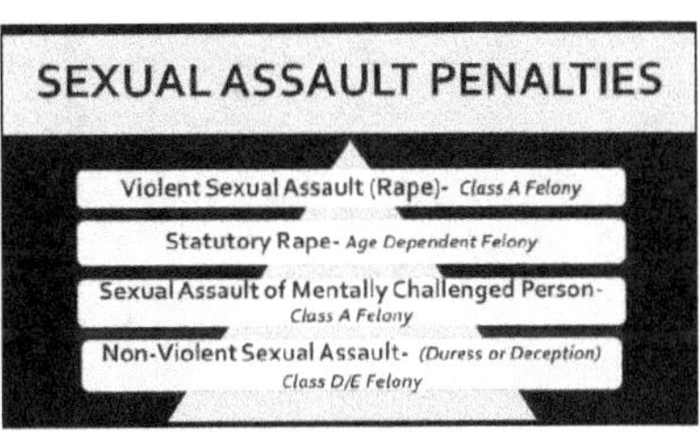

- A non-violent form of sexual assault such as misuse of a power differential or fraud should be a lesser felony and carry a lesser sentence such as a Class D Felony.

Our reproductive system is at the core of our humanity. The anguish of defilement causes intense emotional pain. All victims will need to overcome the tragic consequences of sexual assault in order to recover and survive, but the impact of the assault will affect them throughout their lifetime.

Justice heals. All sexual assault victims, whether violated by a stranger or someone they know and trust, whether defiled in a violent or non-violent way, deserve the healing and validation justice provides.

4

Seven Steps to Conquer Sex Crimes

The United States fought the US Civil War to abolish slavery. Today, we recognize that slavery was a horrific inhumanity and wonder how such an outrageous atrocity could have existed. Yet the fear of abolition pit brother against brother, slaughtering 620,000 soldiers in the process, and ripping our nation apart.

Today, we have people opposed to defining consent as a civil right backed by law because doing so will cause a transformational change. This change will require people to respect human dignity.

In generation after generation, throughout history, men considered women "less than." Our role was to nurture our families and provide entertainment for the men in our lives. We have retained the patriarchal concept of sexual contact in our laws. We all know what consent is until we deal with sexual contact; then our brains dive into the murky zone.

Sex crimes are more common than any form of cancer. In fact, no illness compares with their volume. If we equated sex crimes with a disease, they would be a serious pandemic.

RAINN reports that on average, one American is sexually assaulted every sixty-eight seconds. Victims know their assailant in eight out of ten cases. Approximately 25% of sexual assaults take place in the victim's home. The most vulnerable people in our population are females in their late teens to early thirties, but there is no age limit to sexual assault. Every nine minutes, the victim is a child.

US federal law states that rape is "sexual penetration, no matter how slight, with a body part or object, without the consent of the victim." Without a definition for consent, our military has the highest rate of sexual assault of any jurisdiction in our nation. CAN is currently endeavoring to change that.

Thanks to the efforts of Congresswoman Annie Kuster from New Hampshire, CAN's consent bill was introduced as an amendment to the National Defense Authorization Act (NDAA) that impacts the Uniform Code of Military Justice (UCMJ). It's language also served as the basis for the bill that was introduced in Arkansas. It defines *consent* clearly as a "freely given, knowledgeable and informed agreement by a person with the capacity to reason." CAN will seek approval from both the Senate and the House of Representatives for passage in 2023.

Our lawmakers must hear significant demand from the public in order to create change. Too often, legislators make decisions based on what gets them re-elected vs. what's best for society. Voters must voice their outrage.

Properly defining consent in our laws will alter sexual conduct. People will recognize what causes defilement. They will adjust accordingly rather than risk going to jail or other penalties. Holding people accountable is essential in creating and maintaining a civil society. Sexual conduct will find a new "normal" — one that respects everyone's sexual autonomy.

How YOU can make a difference:

For legislators:

Sponsor a bill to #CodifyConsent in the "General Law" section of penal code for your state or jurisdiction. The noun *consent* is a word with an easily understood definition. Consistency from state to state and location to location is vital for securing society's understanding and conquering rape mentality. CAN will work with you to create this important change. Email: Info@ConsentAwareness.net.

For activists and advocates for change:

CAN fights for consent laws across the US and around the world! Several survivors from high profile cases as well as additional victims and advocates in the US and international locations have rolled up their sleeves to help with this effort. Your support can further the success of CAN's mission. Here are seven ways you can help:

1. Contact CAN to become a Consent Crusader. We will work with you to reach the legislators in your jurisdiction and demand change. Info@ConsentAwareness.net

2. Watch and share my TEDx Talk, *When "Yes" Means "No" — The Truth about Consent* with everyone you know. http://bit.ly/DefineConsent

3. Use the hashtags #FGKIA and #CodifyConsent on your social media wherever you discuss sexual assault, rape, sex trafficking, domestic violence, abortion rights, stealthing, and image based sexual abuse....all acts that rob you of your consent.

4. Watch "Your Consent for Kids," with your children, an entertaining way to give them a consent foundation that will last a lifetime. http://bit.ly/YourConsentForKids

5. Sign the petition to support CAN's pending CONSENT bills at http://bit.ly/BillPetition

6. Donate: We cannot do it alone! We absolutely need your help! https://consentawareness.net/donate

7. Share this information with your entire network.

Consent is a universal issue. Whether you live within the United States or anywhere around the world, adopting the proper definition for consent and removing existing victim-blaming concepts from our penal laws, is crucial in order to make the world a safer place!

FREELY GIVEN, KNOWLEDGEABLE AND INFORMED AGREEMENT, BY A PERSON WITH THE CAPACITY TO REASON!

5

Current Status of Consent in US Penal Law

STATE	STATUS OF CONSENT	PROBLEMS WITH EXISTING LAWS
Alabama	Alabama considers consent to be "acquiescence" or "compliance." Sexual misconduct by fraud is a misdemeanor.	Alabama is a "words and actions" state, with a heavy emphasis on forcible compulsion. "Compliance" is only consent when a freely given, knowledgeable and informed agreement has taken place. "Acquiesence" is agreement under duress, not consent. Alabama provides an extensive list of actions it considers "lack of consent" but does not actually define consent in its statutes.

STATE	STATUS OF CONSENT	PROBLEMS WITH EXISTING LAWS
Alaska	Consent means a freely given, reversible agreement specific to the conduct at issue; in this paragraph, "freely given" means agreement to cooperate in the act was positively expressed by word or action.	Dependence on "word or action" is a blame-the-victim, *Yes Means Yes* concept. Influence, not the "word or action," that results from that influence should determine if consent is present. Alaska's "coercion" only results from force or fear of force. No other types of threat are considered. Consent is revocable, not reversible (see chapter 2). Temporary incapacity applies only when the offender administers the drugs or alcohol.
Arizona	No consent definition.	Lists only specific conducts it deems "without consent" Coercion on applies from force or threat of force. Deception regarding the act but not the actor except when imposter pretends to be the victim's spouse.

STATE	STATUS OF CONSENT	PROBLEMS WITH EXISTING LAWS
Arkansas	No consent definition.	Lists only specific conducts it deems "lack of consent" Coercion is specific to force or fear of force. Deception as to the nature of the act, but not the actor. Incapacity only by nonconsensual administration of intoxicant or substance, or when the victim is unaware the act is taking place.
California	261.1- Consent means "Positive cooperation in act or attitude pursuant to the exercise of free will." The person must act freely and voluntarily and have knowledge of the act or transaction involved.	"Positive cooperation in act or attitude," by the victim may have been influenced by force, duress, deception or exploitation of their incapacity. This *Yes Means Yes* statement enables blame-the-victim defenses. How a victim behaves before, during, and after a sexual assault has no bearing on whether the accused used malicious influence to secure their compliance. Victims should have knowledge of the actor as well as the act.

STATE	STATUS OF CONSENT	PROBLEMS WITH EXISTING LAWS
Colorado	Consent is "Cooperation, act or attitude pursuant to any exercise of free will and with knowledge of the nature of the act." Submission under fear shall not constitute consent.	"Cooperation, act or attitude," can be influenced by force, duress, deception or exploitation of their incapacity. This *Yes Means Yes* statement enables blame-the-victim defenses. How a victim behaves before, during, and after a sexual assault has no bearing on whether the accused used malicious influence to secure their compliance. Victims must have knowledge of the actor as well as the act.
Connecticut	No consent definition- only "lack of consent," including force or threat of force, mental incapacity, mental disability, or physical helplessness.	Lists only specific conducts it deems "lack of consent."
Delaware	No consent definition- only "without consent," including force or threat of force, other coercive means that would compel a reasonable person, mental deficiency, utilization of a ruse by a health practitioner or religious counselor, non-consensual administration of intoxicants or drugs.	Lists only specific conducts it deems "without consent." A person who is intoxicated or drugged, beyond clear thinking, and the accused reasonably should have known, should be off limits regardless of how they got that way.

STATE	STATUS OF CONSENT	PROBLEMS WITH EXISTING LAWS
District of Columbia	"Words or overt actions indicating a freely given agreement to the sexual act or contact in question. Lack of verbal or physical resistance or submission of the victim, resulting from the use of force, threats, or coercion by the defendant shall not constitute consent.	"Words or overt actions" is a victim-blaming, *Yes Means Yes* concept. Although deception by a doctor or during a psychotherapy session is covered, DC's laws protect no other victim of deception. "Words or overt actions" by the victim can be induced by force, duress or deception, or by exploiting incapacity and should not determine if consent takes place. The offender is fully aware that they used malicious influence even when the victim does not know it at the time.
Florida	"Intelligent, knowing, and voluntary consent and does not include coerced submission. Consent shall not be deemed or construed to mean failure by the alleged victim to offer physical resistance to the offender."	Defining the meaning of a word by using the word is confusing. It should read "Intelligent, knowing, and voluntary agreement." Incapacity is not included. Voluntary incapacity due to drugs or alcohol may be prosecuted.
Georgia	No consent definition. Rape is a crime when committed by force or against the will of a female victim.	Lists only specific conducts it will prosecute.

STATE	STATUS OF CONSENT	PROBLEMS WITH EXISTING LAWS
Guam	No consent definition. Using force or threat of violence, overcoming a mentally defective victim, threats of future retaliation, or overcoming the victim by concealment or surprise is a sex crime.	Lists only specific conducts it will prosecute.
Hawaii	No consent definition. Compulsion by force or instilling fear of public humiliation, property damage, or financial loss, is a sex crime.	Lists only specific conducts it will prosecute.
Idaho	No consent definition. Sexual contact with a victim who is unconscious of the nature of the act is a crime. Using pretense or artifice to convince the victim that the offender is their spouse or a different person than who they are is a crime.	Lists only specific conducts it will prosecute. Rape is penile penetration.

STATE	STATUS OF CONSENT	PROBLEMS WITH EXISTING LAWS
Illinois	"Freely given agreement to the act of sexual penetration or sexual conduct in question. • Lack of verbal or physical resistance or submission by the victim resulting from the use of force or threat of force by the accused shall not constitute consent • The manner of dress of the victim at the time shall not constitute consent • A person who initially consented to any sexual penetration or any sexual conduct that occurs after he or she with-draws consent during the course of sexual penetration or sexual conduct is not deemed to have consented."	Fails to state that agreement must be knowledgeable and informed. Agreement is required about the conduct but not about the actor. Threat of force is far from the only type of threat that a malicious predator can use to influence their victim.
Indiana	No consent definition Sexual assault is by force or threat of force, if mentally deficient, if unaware of the conduct, and if attempts to refuse sexual contact are ignored.	Lists only specific conducts it will prosecute and has deliberately refused to address acts of deception. *No Means No* ignores that the victim could be too frightened or incapacitated to say "No," Also, they may have been tricked into compliance.

STATE	STATUS OF CONSENT	PROBLEMS WITH EXISTING LAWS
Iowa	No consent definition. "Sexual abuse" takes place against the victim's will by force, threat of force, when the victim is influenced by a sleep producing drug or is unconscious. Misrepresentation of a medical, therapeutic, or legal nature concerning the act is a sex crime.	Lists only specific conducts it will prosecute and fails to address other acts of deception.
Kansas	No consent definition. Overcoming the victim by forcible compulsion or fear, or if they are unconscious, mentally deficient, younger than 14, or by a ruse that the action is medically necessary or a legal requirement, is a sex crime.	Lists only specific conducts as sex crimes.
Kentucky	No consent definition. Forcible compulsion, incapacity, or if the victim does not expressly or impliedly acquiesce, indicates lack of consent.	Lists only specific conducts as "lack of consent." "Expressly or impliedly acquiesce" is a victim-blaming concept.

STATE	STATUS OF CONSENT	PROBLEMS WITH EXISTING LAWS
Louisiana	No consent definition. Victim must resist the act to the utmost or be prevented from doing so by threats of great and immediate bodily harm, A sex crime is committed when the victim is threatened by a weapon, when under 13, has an IQ of 70 or lower, is a quadriplegic or paraplegic, when resisting the offender's violence would not prevent the rape, when they believe the offender is someone else who is known to them, and when the offender administers a drug or intoxicant without their knowledge.	Lists only specific conduct as criminal offenses.
Maine	No consent definition. Sex crimes take place through force and threat of force and if the other person has not expressly or impliedly acquiesced.	"Expressly or impliedly acquiesced is a *Yes Means Yes,* victim-blaming concept. Lists only specific conducts as criminal "sexual conduct." Considers intoxication or drugs only if administered by the offender.
Maryland	No consent definition A sex crime occurs by force, threat of force, without the (undefined) consent of the person, cognitive impairment, mental incapacity, or when the victim is younger than the age of reason.	Lists only specific conducts as criminal conduct.

STATE	STATUS OF CONSENT	PROBLEMS WITH EXISTING LAWS
Massachusetts	No consent definition Sexual assault occurs by force, against the victim's will, or threat of bodily injury.	Lists only specific conducts as criminal conduct.
Michigan	No consent definition Sexual assault takes place by force or threat of force.	Lists only specific conducts as criminal conduct.
Minnesota	Consent- Words or overt actions by a person indicating a freely given, present agreement to perform a particular sexual act with the actor. Physical helplessness is covered as an offense.	"Words or overt actions" is a victim-blaming *Yes Means Yes,* concept. No matter what you say or do, if the offender used force, fear, fraud or exploited your incapacity, you did not consent. The victim should have the right of consent to the actor as well as the act. Consent is the same in all things, not only sexual contact.
Mississippi	No consent definition	Lists only specific conducts as criminal conduct.

STATE	STATUS OF CONSENT	PROBLEMS WITH EXISTING LAWS
Missouri	No consent definition, but Missouri bases rape on not having (undefined) consent. 2nd degree rape- "Assent is not consent if induced by force, duress or deception." Intoxication, incapacity by drugs only covered if administered without victim's knowledge or consent.	While Missouri states clearly what does not constitute consent, it fails to uphold its own provisions. Refer to the Mario Antoine case, (Chapter 2)
Montana	Overt actions indicating a freely given arrangement to have sexual intercourse or sexual contact through words or actions. Lack of consent may be inferred based on all of the surrounding circumstances and must be considered in determining whether a person gave consent.	Overt actions are a conveyance, but can only convey consent when consent (the noun) is actually taking place. "Overt actions" is a *Yes Means Yes,* victim-blaming concept. Lack of consent should be based on the influence used by the accused, not the, "surrounding circumstances."

STATE	STATUS OF CONSENT	PROBLEMS WITH EXISTING LAWS
Nebraska	No consent definition "Without consent" is determined by force, threat of force, coercion, saying "No," deception as to the actor's identity or the nature of the act. Verbal or physical resistance is not required when the victim feels resistance would be futile. Nebraska identifies force, coercion, and deception as to the identity of the actor or nature of the act as "without consent."	List specific conducts the state will prosecute.
Nevada	Consent is not defined. Sexual assault is "against the will of the victim."	Lists only specific conducts as sexual assaults.
New Hampshire	No consent definition	Lists only specific conducts as "lack of consent."
New Jersey	No consent definition but lists "lack of consent" similar to model penal code: *Consent is ineffective, unless otherwise provided, if it is given by a person who is induced by force, duress, or deception, or by a person who is legally incompetent or otherwise unable to judge the harmfulness of the conduct. N.J.S.A. 2C:2-10c.*	Lists only specific conducts as "lack of consent." New Jersey police and prosecutors have been known to decline prosecution for rape and sexual assault by deception cases.

STATE	STATUS OF CONSENT	PROBLEMS WITH EXISTING LAWS
New Mexico	No consent definition Prosecutes sexual assault for the use of physical force, violence, threat of force, extortion, retaliation, physical punishment, kidnapping, incapacity, misuse of a psychotherapy relationship.	Lists only specific conduct.
New York	No consent definition in penal law; however, sexual assault is conducted "without consent," - which is undefined - but the victim must express their "lack of consent" through their words and actions. This is a *No Means No,* victim-blaming law. Conversely, NY has a *Yes Means Yes* education law called "Affirmative Consent" making "consent" a mutual decision that must be clearly expressed.	Neither *Yes Means Yes* nor *No Means No* is correct.... The influence used by the accused, not the "words and actions" resulting from that influence, determines if consent is actually taking place. The accused knows what influence they used to secure compliance. In addition: Consent is the same in all things, not solely sexual activity. Consent is not "mutual." It is a very personal, singular attitude by a specific individual, and must take place simultaneously with the other agreeing party. Pendingt bills #S6540A and #S6200 will correctly define consent when passed.
North Carolina	No consent definition	Lists only specific conducts as "lack of consent."

STATE	STATUS OF CONSENT	PROBLEMS WITH EXISTING LAWS
North Dakota	No consent definition but it is unlawful to engage in a sexual act when the victim is unaware that a sexual act is being committed. This applies to fraud in the factum cases and if the victim is intoxicated, drugged or otherwise unconscious,	Lists only specific conducts it will prosecute. Fraud covers only fraud in the factum but not fraud in the inducement. If one type of fraud is a weapon in sexual assault, every type of fraud is a weapon in sexual assault.
Ohio	No consent definition	Lists only specific conducts it will prosecute.
Oklahoma	No consent definition	Lists only specific conducts it will prosecute. Deception is a crime when tricking a person into believing the offender is their husband or if they are "unconscious of the nature of the act."
Oregon	No consent definition	Lists only specific conducts it will prosecute.
Pennsylvania	No consent definition- Poor use of the word "acquiesce"	Lists only forcible compulsion or incapacity to consent. Relies on a findlaw.com definition to describe possible defenses against sexual assault charges.

STATE	STATUS OF CONSENT	PROBLEMS WITH EXISTING LAWS
Puerto Rico	No consent definition. Use of trickery, deception, simulation or cover-up regarding the identity of the offender is a crime. Sexual assault includes battery against the bodily or psycho-emotional integrity and dignity of the victim.	Lists only specific acts it will prosecute.
Rhode Island	No consent definition	Lists only specific conducts it will prosecute. Spousal rape is not 1ˢᵗ degree rape
South Carolina	No consent definition	Lists only specific conducts it will prosecute. Limits criminal charges for spousal misconduct.
South Dakota	No consent definition	Lists only specific conducts it will prosecute.
Tennessee	No consent definition but Tennessee identifies force, duress and deception by fraud as "rape."	Lists only specific conducts it will prosecute.

STATE	STATUS OF CONSENT	PROBLEMS WITH EXISTING LAWS
Texas	Section 1.07-11 "Consent means assent in fact whether express or apparent." *Section 1.07-19 "Effective Consent" Consent is not effective if: (A.) induced by force, threat *(duress)* or fraud *(deception.)*	1.07-11 Consent means more than "assent." Assent is agreement on the face of it. Suggested language: "Assent is not consent when induced by force, duress, deception, or by exploiting incapacity. *(as in Rape in the 2nd Degree, Missouri.)* 1.07-19 Indicates what consent is not, but does not indicate what consent is. 1.07 only applies "consent" to theft but not sexual assault.
US Virgin Islands	No consent definition	Lists only specific conducts it will prosecute.
Utah	No consent definition	Lists only specific conducts as "without consent." Posing as the victim's spouse is a crime, but not posing as anyone else.
Vermont	"Words or actions by a person indicating a voluntary agreement to engage in a sexual act."	"Words or actions" is a *Yes Means Yes,* victim-blaming concept. Influence, not the resulting words and actions should determine whether consent did or did not take place. The offender knows if they used malicious influence even if the victim does not know it at the time.

STATE	STATUS OF CONSENT	PROBLEMS WITH EXISTING LAWS
Virginia	No consent definition Sexual battery by ruse is a Class A misdemeanor.	Lists only specific conducts it will prosecute.
Washington	"Actual words or conduct indicating freely given agreement to have sexual intercourse or sexual contact at the time of the act."	"Actual words and conduct" is a *Yes Means Yes,* victim-blaming concept. Influence, not the resulting words and actions should determine whether consent did or did not take place.
West Virginia	No consent definition	Lists only specific conducts as "lack of consent."
Wisconsin	"Words or overt actions by a person who is competent to give informed consent indicating a freely given agreement to have sexual intercourse or sexual contact.	Consent, by its very nature, is "informed." The term "informed consent" is confused terminology. "Words or overt actions" is a *Yes Means Yes,* victim-blaming concept. Influence, not the resulting words and actions should determine whether consent did or did not take place.
Wyoming	No consent definition	Lists only specific conducts it will prosecute.

About the Author

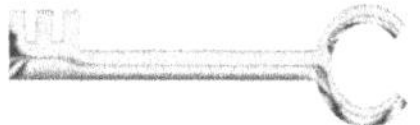

*Y*our Consent, the Key to Conquering Sexual Assault- Revised Edition, is Joyce Short's fourth book on sexual assault. She is the Founder and Chief Executive Officer of the Consent Awareness Network (CAN), an international coalition fighting to define consent properly in our laws.

Ms. Short is a TEDx Talk Presenter and a sexual assault survivor who experienced each form of sexual assault covered by Model Penal Code, by force, duress, and deception. She advocates for survivors, helping them recover their dignity, secure validation, and heal. She conducted in-depth research into rape laws in order to uncover the missing link that enables sex crimes to harm victims in a rampant, unabated fashion, with little or no hope for justice.

The New York State Assembly awarded Ms. Short a "Woman of Distinction" honor. A federal prosecutor in Kansas City, MO, featured her website, currently known as www.ConsentAwareness.net, in the indictment that led to the conviction of a serial rapist with 30+ victims. She wrote the text for and conferred on "consent" bills for several jurisdictions including a US federal amendment to military law. She has testified in legislative hearings in New York, Indiana, Alaska, and more. She has been called on as a *consent* expert witness in sexual assault cases.

Ms. Short has been featured on *Nightline*, the CBS Evening News, ABC, IWomanTV, *BuzzFeed, Inside Edition,* CBC, the Canadian National Radio Station, NYAToday, MNN, *The Newark Star Ledger, VICE, The Kansas City Star,* and additional podcasts and media outlets. She was featured as a speaker in the Women's March as well as for professional conferences, schools, and religious organizations.

Ms. Short is determined to rectify society's concept of consent in order to spare our present and future generations from all nonconsensual sexual acts.

My Consent

My body's not a token, not a prize.
Don't defile me with coercion, force, or lies.
My body's not yours to take; it's mine to give.
My body's not your entitlement; it's where I live.

Don't think consent's a privilege; it's a must,
No matter how intensely you feel lust.
#FGKIA; keep your rape mentality away.
#FGKIA; sign it into law today –

Freely Given, Knowledgeable, and Informed Agreement!

From Ms. Short's TEDx Talk, *When "Yes" Means "No" — The Truth about Consent*, Ursuline Academy, Wilmington Delaware, March 2018.

Standing Firm with Weinstein Survivors at 2020 New York City Hearing:
Louise Godbold, Joyce Short, Katherine Kendall Butler

Harvey Weinstein leaves Manhattan courthouse
with defense team, 2020

Pennsylvania Legislative Briefing: Nina Lucas, Sen. Katie Muth,
Joyce Short, Cheryl Carmel

Cosby Survivors' Vigil, Philadelphia, PA: Joyce Short, Shari Botwin,
Nina Lucas, Tarale Wulff, Aly Marino, Marianne Bustin,
Bird Milliken, Susie Spite-McKinney

Press conference introducing bill #A6540A to the media with NY State Assembly Member Rebecca Seawright and CAN CEO Joyce Short, 2020

Legislative briefing: Joyce Short, IN State Representative Sally Siegrist, and NY State Representative Rebecca Seawright

Legislative Briefing with Consent Crusaders, 2022
Joyce Short, Nina Lucas Harrison, Susie Spite-McKinney, Stacey Pinkerton,
Susan Prout, Dawn Dunning, and Andrea Constand

Joyce Short, Speaker
at Women's March,
New York City, 2021

The Swiss Cheese
Umbrella and
Joyce Short
with Professor
Patricia Moynagh at
Wagner College, Staten
Island, NY. 2020

Joyce Short and
Assembly Member
Rebecca Seawright
featured at abortion
rights rally,
Carl Schurz Park,
New York City,
June 2022

Additional Information

ADDITIONAL WORKS BY JOYCE SHORT:

- *When "Yes" Means "No" — The Truth about Consent,* TEDx Talk at Ursuline Academy, Wilmington Delaware, http://bit.ly/DefineConsent
- *Your Consent for Kids,* You Tube Cartoon, http://bit.ly/YourConsentForKids
- *Carnal Abuse by Deceit,* Available on Amazon, http://bit.ly/CarnalAbuse
- *Combating Romance Scams, Why Lying to Get Laid Is a Crime!* Available on Amazon, http://bit.ly/CombatScams

SOCIAL MEDIA AND CONTACTS:

 Instagram: @yourconsent

 TikTok: @4myconsent

 Facebook: https://www.facebook.com/shortjoyce

 Twitter: @jm_short

 Webpage: http://ConsentAwareness.net

 Email: Info@ConsentAwareness.net